I0797500

ESSENTIAL POEMS

ESSENTIAL POEMS

PAT PARKER

Edited by SaraEllen Strongman

A sapphic classics from
SINISTER WISDOM

Essential Poems by Pat Parker

Editor and Publisher: Julie R. Enszer
Managing Editor: Shawn(ta) Smith-Cruz
Transcription and manuscript assembly: Laura Gibbs

Cover and interior design: Nieves Guerra
Cover photograph: Paula Wallace

Sinister Wisdom, Inc.
2333 McIntosh Road
Dover, FL 33527
sinisterwisdom@gmail.com
www.sinisterwisdom.org

First edition, October 2025

Library of Congress Control Number: 2025939042
ISBN: 978-1-944981-81-5

Printed in the U.S.

Price: 19.95

CONTENTS

INTRODUCTION

In most photos of her performing, Pat Parker is wearing a suit. In my favorite picture of her, she wears a white tie in sharp contrast with a dark shirt and vest. She stands at the microphone, looking off to the side, eyes slightly narrowed. Her right hand is blurry, mid-gesture. I can hear the photo. Her lips are pursed like she has just finished reading a line. I can imagine her waiting a beat for the audience to absorb her words, understand her meaning. Other photos capture her mouth open, book in hand or seemingly finishing an emphatic plosive, hands hovering above a lectern. This is how I think of Parker: in motion, performing.

There are a handful of recordings of Parker reading, including two albums from Olivia Records: *Lesbian Concentrate* and *Where Would I Be Without You*. The latter was a collaboration with her longtime friend and fellow poet Judy Grahn. The recordings confirm what many said about Parker: she was a performance poet. Her voice was deep and sonorous. Her poems, written to be read out loud or, as Cheryl Clarke wrote: "her poetry of political commentary and moral emotions was best encountered *all the way live*" (26, emphasis added). In other photos, in the background of the Gente Gospelaires or performing as part of the Varied Voices of Black Women, Parker is just as vibrant—dancing, gesturing, and living her words within her chosen communities.

The venues where Parker performed reflect her multi-issue, intersectional politics, her involvement in multiple social movements of the 1960s, 70s, and 80s, and her commitment to liberation for all. In her home in the Bay Area, she regularly performed at queer and feminist coffee houses and bars. Her reading tours took her to feminist bookstores and music festivals across the country. In 1976, she read her poem "Womanslaughter" at the International Tribunal on Crimes Against Women in Brussels. Parker also read her work at protests against U.S. imperialism and at fundraisers for incarcerated women. Like her more famous fellow Black lesbian poet and close friend Audre Lorde, Parker refused to leave any part of herself behind, once writing, "The day all the different parts of me can come along, we would have what I would call a revolution." She brought her whole personhood and all of her identities to her poetry, her activism, and her personal life.

Patricia Ann Parker (nee Cook) was born in Houston, TX in 1944. She grew up in a working-class family, as one of five children. In 1962, at the age of seventeen, she left Texas for California. She spent her entire adult life in California, where she made her home and built her career as a poet, teacher, and longtime medical coordinator at the Oakland Women's Health Center. Parker was part of two major literary movements during the 1960s and 1970s: the Black Arts Movement (BAM) and the Women In Print (WIP) movement. The Black Arts Movement was the expressive arm of the Black Power movement.

Black Power's political ideology of self-determination, independence, and racial pride were represented in Black Arts Movement works, and in particular poetry. Parker was a member of the Black Panther Party in Los Angeles and briefly married to Ed Bullins, a BAM playwright and cultural minister of the BPP. She read and was inspired by BAM poets like Nikki Giovanni, and Sonia Sanchez. BAM's influence on Parker's work is evident in her use of anaphora, short lines, and her experimentation with language (spelling, syntax, grammar).

The WIP movement was an effort born out of second-wave feminist organizing to publish and promote work by women writers. From the 1970s through the 1990s, "bookwomen" produced periodicals, ran bookstores, and founded publishers that specialized in women's writing and culture. Parker was deeply embedded in these communities and institutions. She was a member of the Women's Press Collective (WPC), an Oakland-based lesbian feminist publisher. All five of her poetry collections were published by feminist presses. Her first poetry collection *Child of Myself* was published initially by the Bay Area Shameless Hussy Press in 1971. Shameless Hussy published a wide range of feminist work and was the first publisher for Ntozake Shange's *for colored girls*... WPC re-published *Child of Myself* in 1972 and then Parker's second collection *Pit Stop* in 1973. Diana Press published her third collection *Womanslaughter* and the first edition of *Movement in Black*, later editions were rereleased by Crossing Press and Firebrand Books. Firebrand Books also published Parker's final collection *Jonestown & Other Madness* in 1985. Parker built her career as a poet in the feminist arts scene of the Bay Area. She regularly performed her work at feminist and queer venues in the Bay Area like the Women's Building, the lesbian bar Ollie's, and feminist bookstores like Old Wives' Tales. She appeared on billings with other feminist poets like Grahn and Adrienne Rich as well as other lesbian feminist women of color poets including Willyce Kim, Kitty Tsui, Merle Woo, and Cheryl Clarke. Although Parker's early death in 1989 from breast cancer means we only have five poetry collections from her, her body of work is rich and deep and exceeds her published work. This collection highlights her poems, but her archives contain short stories, drafts of plays, and even the beginnings of a memoir and a novel.

I have sat with Parker's work for over a decade now and her words continue to strike deep at my heart. As Lorde once wrote, "Parker's poetry maintains, reaches out and does not let go" (32). I resist traditional scholarly modes of reading poetry and instead read Parker's poems as if she is the speaker simply because so many of them are autobiographical. Her work is powerful in part because it is so fiercely personal. The poems in *Essential Poems by Pat Parker* are ordered chronologically. We chose to organize the poems this way to allow readers to follow the evolution of her voice over more than a decade and recreates how Parker organized her work herself. *Essential Poems* includes poems that represent the major themes and personas in her work: trickster, lesbian, struggling with contradictions, political solidarity, and documentary poetry.

I did not encounter Parker's work in full collections with this kind of context. I first discovered her through the poem "For the White Person Who Wants to Know How to Be My Friend" from her third collection *Womanslaughter.* This poem is a wonderful example of Parker's trenchant wit. It is not a particularly long or flowery poem, nor is it complex metrically or in its imagery. Like much of Parker's work it is forthright about its topic and its views. But it is *funny*. The poem opens immediately with a contradiction: "The first thing you do is to forget that I'm Black/ Second, you must never forget that I'm Black." Paradoxically, the reader is immediately unsure if Parker actually wants any white friends. The poem continues with a list of scenarios and slights, offering guidance for the potential white person who wants to be Parker's friend: "You should be able to dig Aretha, / but don't play her every time i come over." The poem critiques broader society but also the specific versions of racism she encounters in her personal life and within the women's movement. The penultimate stanza critiques sexual racism: "And even if you believe Black are better/ lovers than whites–don't tell me. I start thinking/ of charging stud fees." Parker maintains her reserved, acerbic tone even when describing hurtful comments.

Rather than calling for radical change, this poem addresses the quotidian annoyances of racism. Parker does not ask that others actually change their views, just that they "don't tell [her]." The poem ends on a similarly detached note: "In other words, if you really want to be my/friend–don't make a labor of it. I'm lazy. Remember." Here she invokes the poem's paradoxical opening charge "to forget" and also "to never forget," while also referencing the stereotypical belief that black people are lazy.

This poem is emblematic of Parker's joke or Trickster poems. She deploys a wry, sardonic voice to draw attention to quotidian injustices. Cheryl Clarke describes Parker as a "queer trickster" in her essay "Goat Child and Cowboy" in the reissue of *Movement in Black*. Clarke gives her this designation "[b]ecause of Parker's indeterminacy, her performance of multiple roles, and her interpretive power" (15). She writes, "the tricksters give us the gift of ambiguity–some may call it jive" (17). Like Clarke, I see Parker as a trickster also because of her use of the volta and reversals in her work, her deft wielding of irony. Parker's trickster persona, her ability to shift voice and surprise her audience again and again is part of what makes her work powerful especially when she performed it.

When I introduce people to Parker, I often begin with another of her "trickster" poems, which showcases her acerbic wit and skillful deployment of irony. "For Willyce," which appeared in Parker's second collection and is one of her explicitly lesbian and sexual poems, is an excellent example of Parker's trickster poetry. Written in second-person, it describes what the speaker does, "When i make love to you":

i try
    with each stroke of my tongue
    to say
        i love you
    to tease
        i love you
    to hammer
        i love you

The poem ends describing the speaker's reaction to her lover's ecstatic cries ("oh god! / oh jesus!):

> here it is, some dude's
> getting credit for what
> a woman
> has done
> again.

Parker juxtaposes a description of fierce, insistent lovemaking with the ubiquity of sexism. Even in the intimate space of the bedroom, the patriarchy is inescapable. Parker's criticism comes wrapped in levity, further highlighting the absurdity of reality. Other trickster poems in *Essential Poems* include "To My Vegetarian Friend," "The Law," and "For the Straight Folks Who Don't Mind Gays But Wish They Weren't So BLATANT."

Parker also wrote many poems about lesbian desire. Sometimes categorized as love poems, these works explore the particular contours of lesbian intimacy. The poem "My Lady Ain't No Lady" valorizes non-normative gender performance within lesbian relationships: "my lady is definitely no lady/ which is fine with me." In other poems, Parker describes the pleasure derived from lesbian relationships, and the shame resulting from homophobia. "move in darkness" juxtaposes the "wall of normalcy" during a sexual encounter with a woman with the "sin" and "fear" that the wall temporarily blocks out. Similarly, in "my lover is a woman," Parker describes her relationship with another woman as a safe harbor away from the homophobia and racism she experiences in the outside world:

my lover is a woman
& when i hold her
feel her warmth
    i feel good
    feel safe

Each description of her lover, and the "good" feelings she brings, is followed by a shift: "then–i never think of…" after the shift, Parker lists less pleasant experiences including her family's disapproval or the racial violence that has colored her life since she was a child. Holding both pleasure and pain is a hallmark of Parker's love poems.

As a black lesbian feminist who moved between and across multiple social movements and communities, Parker's life was full of contradictions, which she explored in her poetry. Two poems, "Brother" and "have you ever tried to hide?," level pointed critiques at social movements and organizations. In "Brother," Parker reflects "i don't want to hear/ about/ how *my* real enemy/ is the system." Instead, with another potent reversal, she explains. "that system/ you hit me with/ is called/ a fist." Parker rejects the misogyny sometimes present in the Black Arts Movement's ideology and aesthetics, referencing the physical harm of domestic violence and perhaps also referencing the abuse she suffered during her marriage to Bullins. "have you ever tried to hide?" recounts the similar irony of white feminists' inability to recognize or acknowledge Parker's presence within their women's group, revealing the falseness of the second-wave lexicon of women's solidarity. In another illuminating reversal, Parker drives home the point: "SISTER! your foot's smaller, / but it's still on my neck." As in "Brother," Parker challenges limited understandings of power and oppression that can only hold one axis of power at a time.

Other poems explore successful instances of solidarity across difference. "gente" describes Parker's experiences in a Third World women's group of the same name. Gente was initially founded as a Third World women's softball team. The members had played in a basketball bar league on teams against each other and decided they would prefer to be on a team together. The poem depicts the joy Parker feels as a part of this community of women of color:

It's difficult to explain
  a good feeling
my world has become colorful
  a rainbow of hues
    now
a part of my living
and it feels good.

Parker's "world has become colorful" because this team is a community of women of color. Having this group as "a part of [her] living," a part of her life "feels good." In this community, she can "...talk without worry, / about the racist in the room." In sharp contrast to her experiences in white women's group, like the one described in "have you ever tried to hide?," in gente Parker is "able to say/ *my sisters*/ and not have/ any reservations." The earnest use of "sister" in this poem is the opposite of how Parker deploys it in "have you ever tried to hide?" as an exhortation. Within Gente she feels a sense of belonging that is pleasurable, even joyful. "There is a woman in this town," "Sunday," and "GROUP" also meditate on the ways difference can keep people apart and also bring them together, reflecting both the difficulties and the promises of organizing cross-culturally within the women's liberation movement.

Much of Parker's poetry is documentary. Her early work is deeply autobiographical and traces her childhood experiences, her marriages, and her experience of coming out as a lesbian. Many of her poems address specific events she experienced. "Don't let the fascists speak" was written in response to a demonstration at San Francisco State University in response to an instructor inviting two members of the American Nazi Party to speak to his class. Many of the poems in *Jonestown & Other Madness* document events: "georgia, georgia on my mind" reflects on the Atlanta child murders, the titular poem of the collection explores the causes and aftermath of the massacre at the Peoples Temple Agricultural Project in Guyana, and "on thanksgiving day" contends with Priscilla Joyce Ford's murder of six people in Las Vegas with her car on Thanksgiving in 1980. Parker asserts that all these events are the result of the quotidian violence that shapes our world: racism and sexism and homophobia, and state-sanctioned neglect. Through a structural analysis of violence, Parker can imagine why Priscilla Ford ran people down with her car:

You cannot be insane
to be enraged is not insane
to be filled with hatred is not insane
to lash out at whiteness is not insane
it is being a nigger
it is your place in life.

Parker is aware of how the world can beat a person down, but her trickster mind persists even in these darker poems. Parker with the wry observation that being the second woman executed by the state of Nevada will be Priscilla's "highest finish in life."

By the time *Jonestown* was published, Parker was the mother to two daughters and had founded her own organization the Black Women's Revolutionary Council in 1980. She was reflecting on her years of activism and seeking out new ways to change the world she saw falling apart before her eyes. *Jonestown* concludes with "legacy," a poem she wrote for her daughter with Martha Dunham, Anastasia, who was then two years old. In the poem, Parker responds to those who think her parenting will only "...create an extension/ of perversion." She explains what she has inherited from her parents and grandparents and what she, in turn, hopes to "bequeath" her daughter. Published a mere four years before Parker's early death from breast cancer, the poem's message of generational continuity is especially poignant.

The narrative of Parker's ancestry like her other biographical poems places her as the descendant of poor and working-class Black folk. Her life and struggles are part of a longer history where, "Each generation improves the world/ for the next." Parker intends to continue this tradition with her daughter. In addition to the "strength" she received from her grandparents, and the "pride" "willed" to her by parents, Parker wills her daughter "rage" to confront the "world incomplete" where injustice still reigns. Her life and those of her ancestors before her constitute "a legacy/ of doers/ of people who take risks/ to chisel the crack wider." She charges her daughter to take these gifts:

> Take the strength that you may
> wage a long battle.
> Take the pride that you can
> never stand small.
> Take the rage that you can
> never settle for less.

We inherit this same world. Parker, ever the trickster, shows us through her poems how love can persist despite the horrors, and promises us that "the world incomplete" can be remade. Her moral leadership and her personal vulnerability are a balm and a guide in the present. Her poetry continues to be just as relevant, funny, and sharp as it was when she first performed it.

SaraEllen Strongman
Fall 2025

from *Child of Myself*

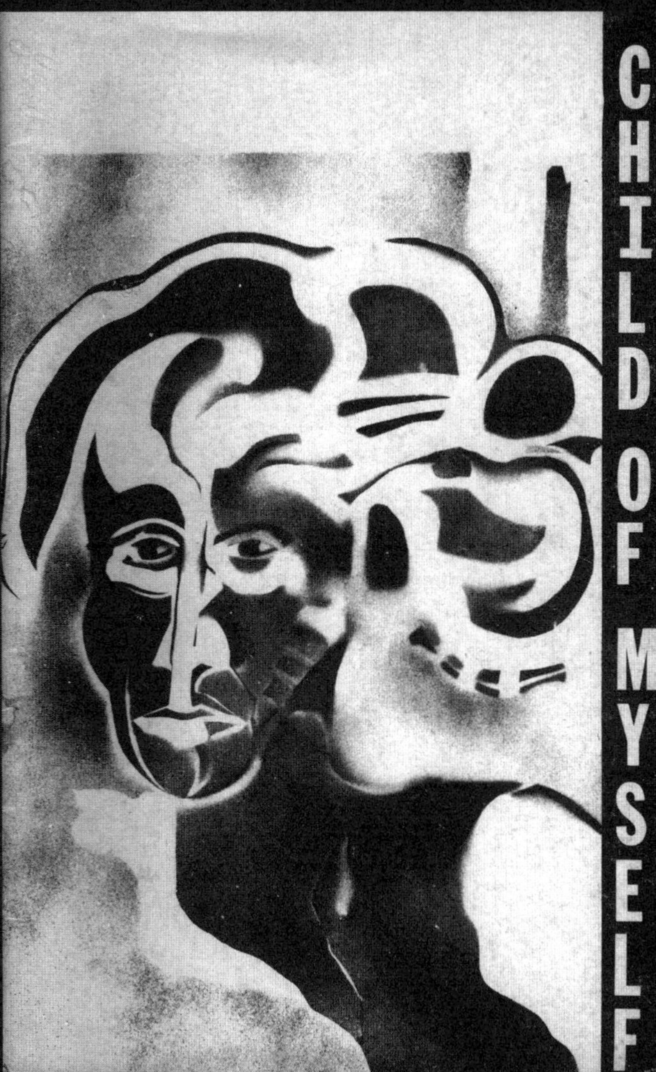

Two covers of *Child of Myself*. The graphic cover is the first edition of *Child of Myself* published by Shameless Hussy Press in 1971, an independent feminist press run by the poet alta. The second cover is from The Women's Press Collective edition in 1974; Parker was a member of The Women's Press Collective and Wendy Cadden, another collective member, designed the image.

This at last is bone of my bones
and flesh of my flesh;
she shall be called Woman,
because she was taken out of
Man.
Genesis 2:23

from cavities of bones
spun
        from caverns of air
i, woman – bred of man
taken from the womb of sleep;
i, woman that comes
before the first.

to think second
to believe first
    a mistake
    erased by the motion of years.
i, woman, i
can no longer claim
    a mother of flesh
    a father of marrow
i, Woman, must be
    the child of myself.

There are two things I've got a
right to, and these are death
or liberty. One or the other
i mean to have.
Harriet Tubman

Brother
I don't want to hear
about
how *my* real enemy
is the system.
i'm no genius,
but i do know
that system
you hit me with
is called
a fist.

EXODUS
(To my husbands, lovers)

a going out or going forth; departure.

Trust me no more –
Our bed is unsafe.
Hidden within folds of cloth
a cancerous rage –

i will serve you no more
in the name of wifely love
i'll not masturbate your pride
in the name of wifely loyalty.

Trust me no more
Our bed is unsafe
Hidden within folds of cloth
a desperate slave

You dare to dismiss my anger
        call it woman's logic
You dare to claim my body
        call it wifely duty.

Trust me no more
Your bed is unsafe
Rising from folds of cloth –

In English Lit.,
        they told me
Kafka was good
        because he created
the best nightmares ever –
I think I should
go find that professor
& ask why
we didn't study
the S.F. Police Dept.

Move in darkness
know the touch of a woman

a wall of normalcy
wraps your body –
strangles
brightens

wrinkled ugliness

sin

fear

admissions

Two days later

you shudder

& take 2 aspirins

FROM DEEP WITHIN

Nature tests those she would calls hers;
Slips up, naked and blank down dark paths.
Skeletons of the sea, this we would become
to suck a ray of sight from the fire.

A woman's body must be taught to speak –
Bearing a lifetime of keys, a patient soul,
moves through a maze of fear and bolts
clothed in soft hues and many candles.

The season's tongues must be heard & taken,
And many paths built for the travelers.
A woman's flesh learns slow by fire and pestle,
Like succulent meats, it must be sucked and eaten.

Let me come to you naked
come without my masks
come dark
        and lay beside you

Let me come to you old
come as a dying snail
come weak
        and lay beside you

Let me come to you angry
come shaking with hate
come callused
        and lay beside you

even more

Let me come to you strong
come sure and free
come powerful

and lay with you.

from
Pit Stop

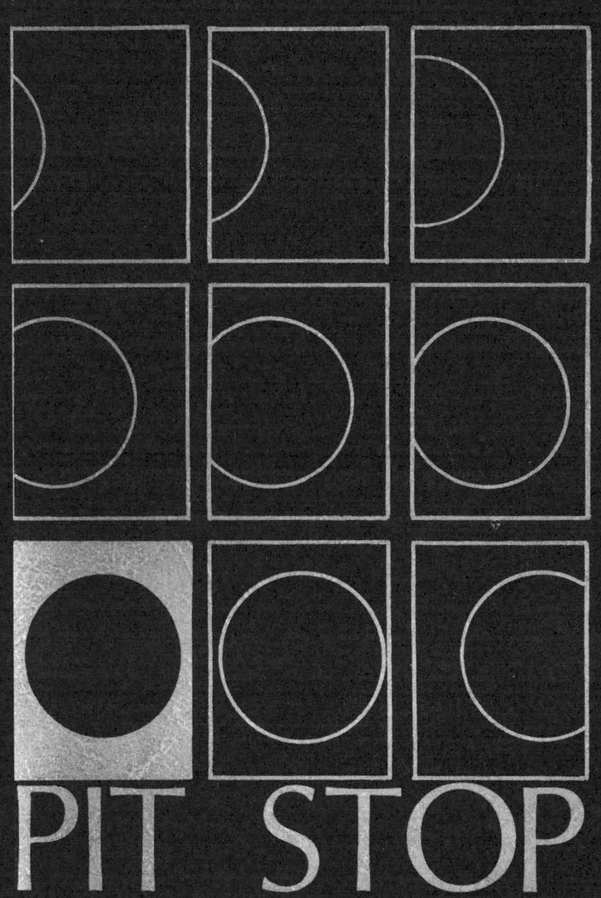

The cover of *Pit Stop*, a chapbook published in 1973 by The Women's Press Collective.

1.
My lover is a woman
    & when i hold her –
        feel her warmth –
        i feel good – feel safe

then/ i never think of
    my families' voices –
    never hear my sisters say –
    bulldaggers, queers, funny –
    come see us, but don't
    bring your friends –
    it's okay with us,
    but don't tell mama
        it'd break her heart
    never feel my father
    turn in his grave
    never hear my mother cry
    Lord, what kind of child is this?

2.

My lover's hair is blonde
    & when it rubs across my face
        it feels soft –
    feels like a thousand fingers
    touch my skin & hold me
    and i feel good.

then/ i never think of the little boy
   who spat & called me a nigger
   never think of the policemen
   who kicked my body and said crawl
   never think of Black bodies
   hanging in trees or filled
   with bullet holes
   never hear my sisters say
   white folks hair stinks
   don't trust any of them
   never feel my father
   turn in his grave
   never hear my mother talk
   of her backache after scrubbing floors
   never hear her cry –
   Lord, what kind of child is this?

3.

My lovers eyes are blue
& when she looks at me
i float in a warm lake
   feel my muscles go weak with want
      feel good – feel safe

Then/ i never think of the blue
   eyes that have glared at me –
   moved three stools away from me
      in a bar
   never hear my sisters rage
   of syphilitic Black men as

guinea pigs –
rage of sterilized children –
watch them just stop in an
intersection to scare the *old*
white bitch.
never feel my father turn
in his grave
never remember my mother
teaching me the yes sirs & mams
to keep me alive –
never hear my mother cry,
Lord, what kind of child is this?

4.

And when we go to a gay bar
& my people shun me because i crossed
the line
& her people look to see what's
wrong with her – what defect
drove her to me –

And when we walk the streets
of this city – forget and touch
or hold hands and the people
stare, glare, frown, & taunt
at those queers –

I remember –
Every word taught to me
Every word said to me

Every deed done to me
& then i hate –
i look at my lover
& for an instant – doubt –

Then/ i hold her hand tighter
And i can hear my mother cry.
Lord, what kind of child is this.

TO AN UNLABELLED

I'm playing a
game.
I don't know the rules.
& I should know,
that's why there are P.E. Majors?
But I'm playing
anyhow

The umpire or referee
or match maker said play.

& you

Jumped in the game.
unlabelled

So who are you.

Sister,
do I call you that.
I hope not.
Sisters are fat ladies
in church,
sweating away sins -
without rumpling their clothes
& keeping me in my place.

His wife - but,
you quit that game

back there,
you changed your uniform.
A regular on the squad

Concert pianist -
I don't know what that means.

I play drums.
but I fake it.
I think that's wrong - but
like I said I don't know the rules.

The game keeper is mad.

Friend?
I've heard that before.
It doesn't quite mean

I call you friend –

&

You know what I mean.

FOR WILLYCE

When i make love to you
i try
with each stroke of my tongue
to say   i love you
to tease   i love you
to hammer   i love you
to melt   i love you

& your sounds drift down
oh god!
oh jesus!
and i think –
here it is, some dude's
getting credit for what
a woman
has done,
again.

BEST FRIENDS (FOR WHITEY)

  So how come
we can't touch
when we hurt most?
  Can only
  sense &
  hurl ourselves
against forces
& each other
& laugh away
our agony
  tomorrow –
as drunk
yesterdays.

Tour America!
a T.V. commercial said.
I will –
there are things I need:
        travelers checks in new york
        gas mask in Berkeley
        face mask in Los Angeles
National guardsmen to protect me
        – in the south
Marines to protect me
        from guardsmen
        – in the mid-west,
Police to protect me
        from hustlers
        – in the ghettos,
Bullet-proof vest and helmet
        to protect me from police
        – everywhere.

Tour America!
perhaps,
        it would be better

to blow it up.

THE *WHAT* LIBERATION FRONT?

Today i had a talk with my dog
he called me a racist – chauvinist person
told me he didn't like the way
i keep trying to change him.
Dogs – he said – do not shit in toilets
Dogs – like to shit outside & he didn't
appreciate being told to shit in the gutter –
just because i didn't like the smell of his shit –
he informed me that the fish weren't so hot
about my shit either.
& property – he wanted to know why
people expected dogs to protect their capitalist interest
he never watches television or plays
records. & how come i put tags on him.
My dog – he laughed. He is his own dog.
And what's this bullshit about his sex
life. If he wants to fuck in the streets it's
his business & the genocide against dogs –
now by this time he's growling – & i just
said – he didn't have to get nasty – i was
willing to study the problem. After all didn't
i buy him good bones and get him groomed
once a month & then he starts hollering
about if he wanted to get dirty &
have long hair that was his right too.
And another thing he said – if he wants to
sit he'll sit – so just shovel my shit about

sit, lie, roll over, stand up. And finally
he said standing up – the next time i patted
him on the head & called him a good boy
he was gonna lift his leg – With that,
he got up & left the house saying something
about a consciousness-raising meeting.

SNATCHES OF A DAY

Grey clouds floated past my window –

    & I ignored them,
    danced into the streets,
    stoned on life.

A woman with brown hair

    like dirty corduroy,
    riding in a Malibu,
    with an olive green suit,
    & a big cigar
    stared at me.
I stopped dancing.

An old cripple dragged past me –

    I offered to carry her;
    She called me a nigger.
        I cut her throat,
        danced around her head,
        sang, "We Shall Overcome"
        hung her scalp over Woolworth's
                        candy counter.

Cops started to arrest me.
    Said I couldn't dance without a permit.
    So, I skipped slowly.

Science teacher lectured for an hour,
    Never did tell me his name,
    So, I didn't tell him mine,
Just my student body & social security numbers.

A friend gave me a God's eye –
    Shocked me,
    Didn't know He had eyes.

My cousin died last week.
    He was a hero.
    Died defending my liberty –
    O sweet liberty,
    Land of the free
    & the great.

Went to a dull movie.
Watched a guy masturbate.

I want to go to sleep.
My cat won't let me under the covers.

SUNDAY

Each Sunday
the people of this town
would go to church
eat dinner
all at one table with their family
the television silent
& bless the food,
father
we thank
THEE
& their maids
off
with their families
& everyone rested
until the Sunday
when the rains
began
and crashed
thru the wind
moving away the dirt
but somebody didn't
stop it
and the
little river
rose
and
rose
till the cars
and televisions

and blankets
and people – all
washed through the
        streets and past
        their neighbors
        for blocks
            and blocks

The troops came on Wednesday
The water had
        stopped
    the wet
merged with the dirt
        mud
                was
        all over
                and
        the troops shook their heads.

They could not
        bury
        the dead.

In the
        death murk

they could not tell
        the
        Black
        from
        the white.

QUESTIONS

"Until all oppressed people
are free –
none of us are free."

I.

the chains are different now –
lay on this body strange
no metal clanging in my ears

chains laying strange
chains laying light-weight
laying credit cards
laying welfare forms
laying buying time
laying white packets of dope
laying afros & straightened hair
laying pimp & revolutionary
laying mother & daughter
laying father & son

chains laying strange –
strange laying chains
        chains

        how do i break these chains

II.

the chains are different now –
laying on this body strange
funny chains – no clang
chains laying strange
chains laying light-weight
chains laying dishes
chains laying laundry
chains laying grocery markets
chains laying no voice
chains laying children
chains laying selective jobs
chains laying less pay
chains laying girls & women
chains laying wives & women
chains laying mothers & daughters

chains laying strange
strange laying chains
          chains

how do i break these chains

III.

the chains are still here
laying on this body strange
no metal – no clang
chains laying strange
chains laying light-weight

chains laying funny
chains laying different
chains laying dyke
chains laying bull-dagger
chains laying pervert
chains laying no jobs
chains laying more taxes
chains laying beatings
chains laying stares
chains laying myths
chains laying fear
chains laying revulsion

chains laying strange
strange laying chains
        chains

how do i break these chains

IV.

the chains are here
no metal – no clang
chains of ignorance & fear
chains here – causing pain

how do i break these chains
to whom or what
do i direct pain
        Black – white
        mother – father

sister – brother
straight – gay

how do i break these chains
how do i stop the pain
who do I ask – to see
what must i do – to be free

sisters – how do i break your chains
brothers – how do i break your chains
mothers – how do i break your chains
fathers – how do i break your chains

i don't want to kill –
i don't want to cause pain –

how –
how else do i break – your chains

How do we know that the panthers
will accept a gift from
white – middle – class – women?

Have you ever tried to hide?
In a group
of women
hide
yourself
slide between the floor boards
slide yourself away child
away from this room
& your sister
before she notices
your Black self &
her white mind
slide your eyes
down
away from the other Blacks
afraid – a meeting of eyes
& pain would travel between you –
change like milk to buttermilk
a silent rage.
SISTER! your foot's smaller,
but it's still on my neck.

Boots are being polished
Trumpeters clean their horns
Chains and locks forged
The crusade has begun.

Once again flags of Christ
are unfurled in the dawn
and cries of soul saviors
sing apocalyptic on air waves.

Citizens, good citizens all
parade into voting booths
and in self-righteous sanctity
X away our right to life.

I do not believe as some
that the vote is an end.
I fear even more
It is just a beginning.

So I must make assessment
Look to you and ask:
Where will you be
when they come?

They will not come
a mob rolling
through the streets

but quickly and quietly
move into our homes
and remove the evil,
the queerness,
the faggotry,
the perverseness
from their midst.
They will not come
clothed in brown
and swastikas, or
bearing chests heavy   with
gleaming crosses.
The time and   need
for ruses are   over.
They will come
in business suits
to buy your homes
and bring bodies to
fill your jobs.
They will come in robes
to rehabilitate
and white coats
to subjugate
and where will you be
when they come?

Where will we *all be*
when they come?
And they will come –

they will come
because we are

defined as opposite –
perverse
and we are perverse.

Every time we watched
a queer hassled in the
streets and said nothing –
It was an act of perversion.

Every time we lied about
the boyfriend or girlfriend
at coffee break –
It was an act of perversion.

Every time we heard,
"I don't mind gays
but why must they
be blatant?" and said nothing –
It was an act of perversion.

Every time we let a lesbian mother
lose her child and did not fill
the courtrooms –
It was an act of perversion.

Every time we let straights
make out in bars while
we couldn't touch because
of laws –
It was an act of perversion.

Every time we put on the proper
clothes to go to a family

wedding and left our lovers
at home –
It was an act of perversion.

Every time we heard
"Who I go to bed with
is my personal choice –
it's personal not political"
and said nothing –
It was an act of perversion.

Every time we let our straight relatives
bury our dead and push our
lovers away –
It was an act of perversion.

And they will come.
They will come for
the perverts

& it won't matter
if you're
        homosexual, not a faggot
        lesbian, not a dyke
        gay, not queer
It won't matter
if you
        own your business
        have a good job
        or are on S.S.I.
It won't matter

if you're
        Black
        Chicano
        Native American
        Asian
        or White

It won't matter
if you're from
        New York
        or Los Angeles
        Galveston
        or Sioux Falls
It won't matter
if you're
        Butch, or Fem
        Not into roles
        Monogamous
        Non Monogamous
It won't matter
If you're
        Catholic
        Baptist
        Atheist
        Jewish
        or M.C.C.

They will come
They will come
to the cities
and to the land

to your front rooms
and in *your* closets.

They will come for
the perverts
and where will
you be
When they come?

i have a dream
  no –
  not Martin's
though my feet moved
  down many paths.
it's a simple dream –

i have a dream
  not the dream of the vanguard
  not to turn this world –
    all over
  not the dream of the masses
not the dream of women
    not to turn this world
      all
        over
it's a simple dream –

In my dream –
  i can walk the streets
    holding hands with my lover

In my dream –
 i can go to a hamburger stand
 & not be taunted by bikers on a holiday

In my dream –
  i can go to a public bathroom,
  & not be shrieked at by ladies –

In my dream –
    i can walk ghetto streets
    & not be beaten up by my brothers.

In my dream –
    i can walk out of a bar
    & not be arrested by the pigs

I've placed this body
    placed this mind
    in lots of dreams –
    in Martin's & Malcolm's –
    in Huey & Mao's –
    in George & Angela's –
    in the north & south
                of Vietnam & America
                        & Africa

i've placed this body & mind
    in dreams –
    dreams of people –

now i'm tired –
now you listen!
    i have a dream too.
    it's a simple dream.

from *Womanslaughter*

The cover of the 1978 edition of *Womanslaughter*, published by Diana Press in Oakland, California. Irmagean made the cover image.

GROUP

"The primary lesson learned by any
minority is self-hatred."

I do not know
when my lessons began

I have no memory –
    of a teacher,
    or books.

osmosis – perhaps
the lessons slip
into my brain
my cells – silently

I do have memory of
childhood chants

if you're white – alright
if you're brown – stick around
if you're Black – get back

I do have memory of teachers

"you are heathens
why can't you be
like the white kids
you are bad – "

    Bad

& I never thought
to ask the Black teachers
in the all-Black schools
how did they know
how white kids were?

Bad

I do have memory
of playground shouts
"your lips are too big"
a memory of my sisters
putting on lipstick
on half of their lips
to make them look smaller

Bad

"your hair nappy"
I do have memory
of "Beauty" parlours
& hot combs and grease

Bad

*"stay out of the sun
it'll make you darker"*
I do have memory
of Black & White
bleaching cream
Nadinola
Bleach & Glow

Bad

"your nose is too big"
I do have memory
of mothers pinching
their babies' noses
to make them smaller
        Bad
        BAD
I do not know
when my lessons
        began
do not know
when my lessons
        were learned,
absorbed into my cells

        now
there are new lessons
        new teachers
each week I go to my group
        see women
                    Black women
Beautiful Black Women
& I am in love
                    with each of them
& this is important
        in the loving
in the act of loving
        each woman
I have learned a new lesson
I have learned
        to love myself

GENTE

It's difficult to explain
a good feeling –
my world has become colorful –
a rainbow of hues
now – a part of my living
          and it feels good.

it feels good
to listen to people
talk about the streets
& know
it's not a *vicarious* experience.

it feels good
to sit and be loose
to talk, without worry,
about the racist in the room.

it feels good
to hear
'we're gonna have a party'
& know it's really
going to be a party.

it feels good
to be able to say
my sisters
and not have
any reservations.

But best of all –
it feels good
to sit in a room
and say
'Have you ever felt like...?'
and somebody has.

FOR THE WHITE PERSON WHO WANTS TO KNOW HOW TO BE MY FRIEND

The first thing you do is to forget that i'm Black.
Second, you must never forget that i'm Black.

You should be able to dig Aretha,
but don't play her every time i come over.
And if you decide to play Beethoven – don't tell me
his life story. They made us take music appreciation too.

Eat soul food if you like it, but don't expect me
to locate your restaurants
or cook it for you.

And if some Black person insults you,
mugs you, rapes your sister, rapes you,
rips your house, or is just being an ass –
please, do not apologize to me
for wanting to do them bodily harm.
It makes me wonder if you're foolish.

And even if you really believe Blacks are better lovers than
whites – don't tell me. I start thinking of charging stud fees.

In other words – if you really want to be my friend – *don't*
make a labor of it. I'm lazy. Remember.

TO MY VEGETARIAN FRIEND

It's not called soul food
because it goes with music.
It is a survival food.

        from the grease
sprang generations
of my people
            generations
        of slaves
that ate the leavings
        of their masters
                & survived

And when I sit –
faced by
chitterlins & greens
neckbones & tails
it is a ritual –
it is a joining –
me to my ancestors
& your words ring untrue
this food is good for me
It replenishes my soul

so if you really
can't stand
to look at my food
can't stand

to smell my food
& can't keep those feelings
        to yourself

Do us both a favor
& stay home

"Don't let the fascists speak."
"We want to hear what they have to say."
"Keep them out of the classroom."
"Everybody is entitled to freedom of speech."

I am a child of America
a step child
        raised in the back room
yet taught
        taught how to act
in her front room.
my mind jumps
the voices of students
screaming
insults   threats
"Let the Nazis speak"
"Let the Nazis speak"
Everyone is entitled
        to speak
I sit a greasy-legged
        Black child
in a Black school
in the Black part of town
look to a Black teacher
the Bill of Rights
        guarantees
us all the right
        my mind

remembers   chants
article I   article I
& my innards churn
they remember
the Black teacher
in the Black school
in the Black part
of the very white town
who stopped us
when we attacked
the puppet principal
the white Board
of mis-Education
cast-off books
illustrated with
cartoons &
words of wisdom
written by white
children in the
other part of town
missing pages
caricatures
of hanging niggers –
the bill of rights
was written to
          protect
               us

my mind remembers
& my innards churn
conjure images

police
break up
illegal demonstrations
illegal assemblies
conjure image
of a Black Panther
"if tricky Dick
tries to stop us
we'll stop him."
conjure image
of that same Black man
going to jail
for threatening
the life of
THE PRESIDENT
every citizen
is entitled to
freedom of speech
my mind remembers
& my innards churn
conjure images
of jews in camps—
of homosexuals in camps—
of socialists in camps—
"Let the Nazis speak"
"Let the Nazis speak"
faces in a college
classroom
"You're being fascist too."
"We want to hear what
they have to say"

faces in
a college classroom
young white faces
speak let them speak
speak let them speak
Blacks jews some whites
seize the bullhorn
"We don't want to hear
your socialist rhetoric"
socialist rhetoric
survival
rhetoric
the supreme court
says it is illegal
to scream fire
in a crowded theater
to scream fire
in a crowded theater
causes people to panic
to run to hurt each other
my mind remembers
& now i know
what my innards
say
illegal to cause
people
to panic
to run
to hurt
there is
no contradiction

what the Nazis say
will cause
        people
        to hurt
        ME.

WHERE DO YOU GO TO BECOME A NON-CITIZEN?

I want to resign; I want out.
I want to march to the nearest place
Give my letter to a smiling face.
I want to resign; I want out.

President Ford vetoed a jobs bill
Sent to him from capitol hill
While we sit by being super cool
He gets a $60,000 swimming pool.
I wanna resign; I want out.

$68,000 to Queen Elizabeth to not grow cotton.
Yet there's no uproar that this jive is rotten.
$14,000 to Ford Motors to not plant wheat
I guess the government don't want wheat all over
    the seats.
I wanna resign; I want out.

The CIA Commission was in session for 26 weeks long
Said the boys didn't do too much wrong
They gave out acid – a test – they tell
Yet if you and I used it – we'd be in jail.
I wanna resign; I want out.

And from Taft College – a small group of fools
Chased all the Black students out of the school.
And good citizens worried about property sale
Chased away Black teenagers from picturesque Carmel.
I wanna resign; I want out.

The Little League after using all excuses up
Says a 10-year-old-girl must use a boy's supportive cup.
An international Women's Congress in Mexico to make plans
Elected for their president – a white-liberal man.
I wanna resign; I want out.

The A.P.A. finally said all gays aren't ill
Yet ain't no refunds on their psychiatry bills.
A federal judge says MCC is valid – a reality
Yet it won't keep the pigs from hurting you or me.
I wanna resign; I want out.

I wanna resign; I want out.
Please lead me to the place
Show me the smiling face
I'm skeptical – full of doubt.
I wanna resign; I want out.

FOR THE STRAIGHT FOLKS WHO DON'T MIND GAYS BUT WISH THEY WEREN'T SO BLATANT

you know some people
got a lot of nerve.
sometimes, i don't believe
the things i see and hear.

Have you met the woman
who's shocked by 2 women kissing
& in the same breath,
tells you that she's pregnant?
BUT GAYS SHOULDN'T BE BLATANT.

Or this straight couple
sits next to you in a movie
& you can't hear the dialogue
Cause of the sound effects.
BUT GAYS SHOULDN'T BE BLATANT.

And the woman in your office
Spends the entire lunch hour
talking about her new bikini drawers
& how much her husband likes them.
BUT GAYS SHOULDN'T BE BLATANT.

Or the "hip" chick in your class,
rattling a mile a minute –
while you're trying to get stoned
in the john

about the camping trip she took
with her musician boyfriend.
BUT GAYS SHOULDN'T BE BLATANT.

You go in a public bathroom
and all over the walls
there's John loves Mary,
Janice digs Richard,
Pepe loves Delores, etc. etc.
BUT GAYS SHOULDN'T BE BLATANT.

Or you go to an amusement park
& there's a tunnel of love
& pictures of straights
painted on the front
& grinning couples
coming in and out.
BUT GAYS SHOULDN'T BE BLATANT.

Fact is, blatant heterosexuals
are all over the place.
Supermarkets, movies, on your job,
in church, in books, on television
every day and night, every place –
even in gay bars.
& they want gay men & women
to go hide in the closets –

So to you straight folks
i say – Sure, i'll go
if you go too,
but i'm polite
so – after you.

MY LADY AIN'T NO LADY

my lady ain't no lady
she doesn't flow into a room –
she enters & her presence is felt.
she doesn't sit small –
she takes her space.
she doesn't partake of meals –
she eats – replenishes herself

my lady ain't no lady –

she has been known
    to speak in a loud voice,
    to pick her nose,
    stumble on a sidewalk,
    swear at her cats,
    swear at me,
    scream obscenities at men,
    paint rooms,
    repair houses,
    tote garbage,
    play basketball,
    & numerous other
    un ladylike things.

my lady is definitely no lady
which is fine with me,

cause i ain't no gentleman.

there is a woman in this town

she goes to different bars
sits in the remotest place
watches the other people
drinks til 2 & goes home - alone

some say she is lonely
some say she is an agent
none of us speak to her

Is she our sister?

there is a woman in this town
she lives with her husband
she raises her children
she says she is happy
& is not a women's libber

some say she is mis-guided
some say she is an enemy
none of us know her

Is she our sister?

there is a women in this town

she carries a lot of weight
her flesh triples on her frame

she comes to all the dances
dances a lot; goes home – alone

some say she's a lot of fun
some say she is too fat
none of us have loved her

Is she our sister?

there is a woman in this town

she owns her own business
she goes to work in the day
she goes home at night
she does not come to the dances

some say she is a capitalist
some say she has no consciousness
none of us trust her

Is she our sister?

there is a woman in this town

she comes to all the parties
wears the latest men's fashions
calls the women mama
& invites them to her home

some say she's into roles
some say she hates herself
none of us of us go out with her

Is she our sister?

there is a woman in this town

she was locked up
she comes to many meetings
she volunteers for everything
she cries when she gets upset

some say she makes them nervous
some say she's too pushy
none of us invite her home

Is she our sister?

there is a woman in this town

she fills her veins with dope
goes from house to house to sleep
borrows money wherever
she can she pays it back if she must

some say she is a thief
some say she drains their energy
none of us have trusted her

Is she our sister?

once upon a time, there was a dream
a dream of women. a dream of women
coming together and turning the world

around. turning the world around and making it over
a dream of women, all women being sisters.
a dream of caring; a dream of protection, a dream
of peace.

once upon a time, there was a dream
a dream of women. for the women who rejected the
dream; there had only been a reassurance. for the
women who believed the dream – there is dying, women,
sisters dying
    once upon a time there was a dream, a dream of women
turning the world all over, and it still lives –
it lives for those who would be sisters.

it lives for those who need a sister
it lives for those who once upon a time had a dream.

THE LAW

In my youth
i was taught
the law is good –
my parents,
my teachers,
    all
told of policemen
to help me find my way –
of courts, to punish
those who would harm me
i was taught
"respect the law"
Now, in my third decade
I have seen the law

the law
comes to homes
& takes the poor
for traffic tickets
the law
takes people to jail
for stealing food
the law
comes in mini-skirts
to see if your home
is bare enough
for welfare
the law

sits in robes
in courtrooms
& takes away
your children
the law
arrests the prostitute
but not her customer
the law
sends a rich woman
to jail on weekends
for murder
sends a porno bookseller
to jail for 30 years
the law
tries women who kill
rapists &
frees the rapist
because rape
is a "normal"
reaction
And my mind reels
    contradictions
    contra/
        dictions
& the voices from
my youth declare

the law is good
the law is *fair*
the law is *just*
& then I realize

good, fair, just,
are all 4 letter words
& to use 4 letter words
is against the law

WOMANSLAUGHTER

It doesn't hurt as much now –
the thought of you dead
doesn't rip at my innards,
leaves no holes to suck rage.
Now, thoughts of the four
daughters of Buster Cooks,
children, survivors
of Texas Hell, survivors
of soul-searing poverty,
survivors of small town
mentality, survivors
now three
doesn't hurt as much.

I.

An Act

I used to be fearful
of phone calls in the night –
never in the day.

Death, like the vampire,
fears the sun
never in the day –
"Hello, Patty."
"Hey, big sister

what's happening?
How's the kids?"
"Patty, Jonesy shot Shirley,
She didn't make it."

Hello, Hello Death
Don't you know it's daytime?
The sun is much too bright today
Hello, Hello Death
you made a mistake
came here too soon, again.
Five months, Death
My sisters and I just met
in celebration of you –
We came, the four strong
daughters of Buster Cooks,
and buried him –
We came, the four strong
daughters of Buster Cooks,
and took care of his widow.
We came, the four strong
daughters of Buster Cooks
and shook hands with his friends.
We came, the four strong
daughters of Buster Cooks,
and the right flowers.
We came, the four strong
daughters of Buster Cooks,
walked tall & celebrated you.
We came, his four strong daughters,
and notified insurance companies

arranged social security payments
gathered the sum of his life.

"We must be strong for mother."

She was the third daughter of Buster Cooks.
I am the fourth.
And in his death we met.
The four years that separated us – gone.
And we talked.
She would divorce the quiet man.
Go back to school – begin again.
Together we would be strong
& take care of Buster's widow.
The poet returned to the family.
The fourth daughter came home.

Hello, Hello Death
What's this you say to me?
Now there are three.
We came, the three sisters
of Shirley Jones
& took care of her mother.
We picked the right flowers,
contacted insurance companies,
arranged social security payments,
and cremated her.
We came, the three sisters
of Shirley Jones.
We were not strong.
"It is good, they said,
that Buster is dead.

He would surely kill
the quiet man."

II.

Justice

There was a quiet man
He married a quiet wife
Together, they lived
a quiet life.

Not so, not so
her sisters said,
the truth comes out
as she lies dead.
He beat her.
He accused her
of awful things
& he beat her.
One day she left.

"Hello, Hello Police
I am a woman
& I am afraid
My husband means to kill me."

She went to her sister's house
she, too, was a woman alone.
The quiet man came & beat her.
Both women were afraid.

"Hello, Hello Police
I am a woman
& I am afraid.
My husband means to kill me."

The four strong daughters
of Buster Cooks
came to bury him –
the third one carried a gun.
"Why do you have a gun?"
"For protection – just in case."
"Can you shoot it?"
"Yes, I have learned well."

"Hello, Hello Police
I am a woman alone
& I am afraid.
My husband means to kill me."

"Lady, there's nothing we can do
until he tries to hurt you.
Go to the judge & he will decree
that your husband leaves you be."
She found an apartment
with a friend.
She would begin
a new life again.
Interlocutory Divorce Decree in hand;
The end of the quiet man.
He came to her home

& he beat her.
Both women were afraid.

"Hello, Hello Police
I am a woman alone
& I am afraid.
My ex-husband means to kill me."

"Fear not, lady,
he will be sought."
It was *too* late
when he was caught.
One day a quiet man
shot his quiet wife
three times in the back.
He shot her friend as well.
His wife died.

The three sisters
of Shirley Jones
came to cremate her.
They were not strong.

III.

Somebody's Trial

"It is good, they said,
that Buster is dead.
He would surely kill
the quiet man."

I was not at the trial.
I was not needed to testify.
She slept with other men, he said.
No, said her friends.
No, said her sisters.
That is a lie.
She was Black.
You are white.
Why were you there?
We were friends, she said.
I was helping her move
the furniture; the divorce court
had given it to her
Were you alone? they asked.
No two men came with us.
They were gone with a load.
She slept with women, he said.
No, said her sisters.
No, said her friends.
We were only friends.
That is a lie.
You lived with this woman?
Yes, said her friend.
You slept in the same bed?
Yes, said her friend.
Were you lovers?
No, said her friend.
But you slept in the same bed?
Yes, said her friend.

What shall be done with this man?
Is it a murder of the first degree?
No, said the men,

It is a crime of passion.
He was angry.
Is it a murder of the second degree?
Yes, said the men,
but we will not call it that.
We must think of his record.
We will call it manslaughter.
The sentence is the same.
What will we do with this man?
His boss, a white man came.
This is a quiet Black man, he said.
He works well for me
The men sent the quiet
Black man to jail.
He went to work in the day.
He went to jail & slept at night.
In one year, he went home.

IV.

Woman-slaughter

"It is good, they said,
that Buster is dead.
He would surely kill
the quiet man."

Sister, I do not understand.
I rage & do not understand.
In Texas, he would be freed.
One Black kills another

One less Black for Texas.
But this is not Texas.
This is California.
The city of angels.
Was his crime so slight?
George Jackson served
years for robbery.
Eldridge Cleaver served
years for rape.
I know of a man in Texas
who is serving 40 years
for possession of marijuana.
Was his crime so slight?
What was his crime?
He only killed his wife.
But a divorce I say.
Not final, they say;
Her things were his
including her life.
Men cannot rape their wives.
Men cannot kill their wives.
They passion them to death.

The three sisters
of Shirley Jones
came & cremated her
& they were not strong.
Hear me now –
it is almost three years
& I am again strong.
I have gained many sisters.
And if one is beaten,

or raped, or killed,
I will not come in mourning black.
I will not pick the right flowers.
I will not celebrate her death
& it will matter not
if she's Black or white –
if she loves women or men.
I will come with my many sisters
and decorate the streets
with the innards of those
brothers in womenslaughter.
No more, can I dull my rage
in alcohol & deference
to *men's* courts.
I will come to my sisters,
not dutiful,
I will come strong.

from *Movement in Black*

Four covers of *Movement in Black*. The cover in the upper left is the cover of the 1978 cloth edition published by Diana Press in Oakland, California; the image is of the sculpture *Black Unity* by Elizabeth Catlett. The cover in the upper right is the cover of the 1983 edition from The Crossing Press. The cover in the lower left is the cover of the 1989 posthumous edition from Firebrand Books in Ithaca, New York; the cover was designed by Betsy Bayley. The cover in lower right is the 1999 expanded edition published by Firebrand Books; the cover was designed by Debra Engstrom. Marilyn Humphries made the photograph of Parker on both of the Firebrand editions.

MOVEMENT IN BLACK

Movement in Black
movement in Black
can't keep em back
movement in Black

I.

They came in ships
from a distant land
bought in chains
to serve the man

I am the slave
that chose to die
I jumped overboard
& no one cried

I am the slave
sold as stock
walked to and fro
on the auction block

They can be taught
if you show them how
they're strong as bulls
and smarter than cows.

I worked in the kitchen
cooked ham and grits

seasoned all dishes
with a teaspoon of spit.

I worked in the fields
picked plenty of cotton
prayed every night
for the crop to be rotten.

All slaves weren't treacherous
that's a fact that's true
but those who were
were more than a few.

Movement in Black
Movement in Black
Can't keep em back
Movement in Black

II.

I am the Black woman
& I have been all over
when the colonists
fought the British
i was there
i aided the colonist
i aided the British
i carried notes,
stole secrets,
guided the men
& nobody thought

to bother me
i was just a
Black woman
the britishers lost
and I lost,
but I was there
& I kept on moving

I am the Black woman
& i have been all over
i went out west, yeah
the Black soldiers
had women too,
& i settled the land,
& raised crops & children,
but that wasn't all

I hauled freight,
& carried mail,
drank plenty whiskey
shot a few men too.
books don't say much
about what I did
but I was there
& I kept on moving.

I am the Black woman
& i have been all over
up on platforms & stages
talking about freedom
freedom for Black folks

freedom for women
In the civil war too
carrying messages,
bandaging bodies
spying and lying
the south lost
& i still lost
but I was there
& i kept on moving

I am the Black woman
& I have been all over
I was on the bus
with Rosa Parks
& in the streets
with Martin King
I was marching
and singing
and crying
and praying

I was with SNCC
& i was with CORE
I was in Watts
when the streets
were burning
I was a panther
in Oakland
in new york
with N.O.W.
In San Francisco
with gay liberation

in D.C with
the radical dykes
yes, I was there
& i'm still moving

movement in Black
movement in Black
can't keep em back
movement in Black

III.

I am the Black woman

I am Bessie Smith
singing the blues
& all the Bessies
that never sang a note

I'm the southerner
who went north
I'm the northerner
who went down home

I'm the teacher
in the all-Black school
I'm the graduate
who cannot read

I'm the social worker
in the city ghetto

I'm the car hop
in a delta town

I'm the junkie with a jones
I'm the dyke in the bar
I'm the matron at a county jail
I'm the defendant with nothin' to say.

I'm the woman with 8 kids
I'm the woman who didn't have any
I'm the woman who's poor as sin
I'm the woman who's got plenty

I'm the woman who
raised white babies &
taught my kids to
raise themselves.

movement in Black
movement in Black
can't keep em back
movement in Black

IV.

Roll call, shout em out

Phillis Wheatley
Sojourner Truth
Harriet Tubman
Frances Ellen Watkins Harper

Stagecoach Mary
Lucy Prince
Mary Pleasant
Mary McLeod Bethune
Rosa Parks
Coretta King
Fannie Lou Hamer
Marian Anderson
& Billies
& Bessie
sweet Dinah
A-re-tha
Natalie
Shirley Chisholm
Barbara Jordan
Patricia Harris
Angela Davis
Flo Kennedy
Zora Neal Hurston
Nikki Giovanni
June Jordan
Audre Lorde
Edmonia Lewis
and me
and me
and me
and me
and me
& all the names we forgot to say
& all the names we didn't know
& all the names we don't know, yet.

movement in Black
movement in Black
Can't keep em back
movement in Black

V.

I am the Black woman
I am the child of the sun
the daughter of dark
I carry fire to burn the world
I am water to quench its throat
I am the product of slaves
I am the offspring of queens

I am still as silence
I flow as the stream

I am the Black woman
I am a survivor
I am a survivor
I am a survivor
I am a survivor
I am a survivor

Movement in Black.

from
Jonestown & Other Madness

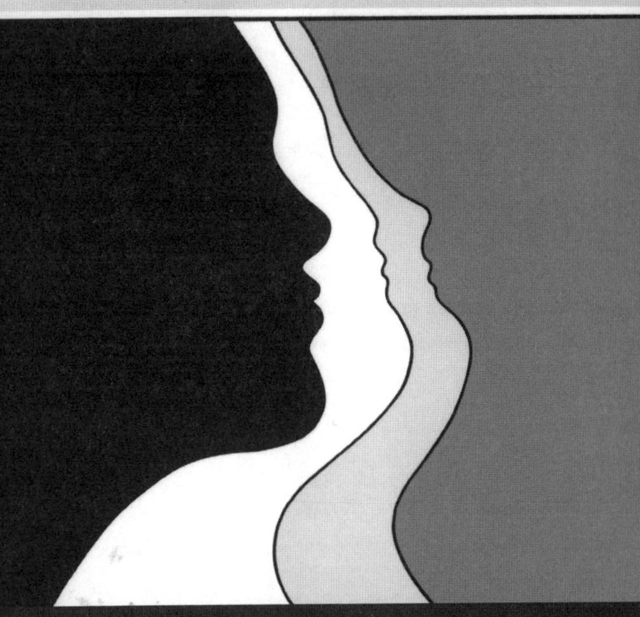

The cover of *Jonestown & Other Madness* published in 1985 by Firebrand Books. Cover design by Cassandra Maxwell-Simmons and Betsy Bayley.

BAR CONVERSATION

Three women were arrested for
assault recently after they beat
up a woman who put a swastika
on another woman's shoulder during
a S & M encounter

It's something you should write about.
If you talk about it
then women will listen
and know it's ok.
Now, envision one poet sitting in a bar
not cruising
observing the interactions
and then sitting face to face
with a young woman
who wants a spokesperson for
sado-masochism
among lesbians.
The first impulse is to dismiss
the entire conversation as more
ramblings of a *SWG*

(read Silly White Girl:
derogatory
characterization
used by minorities for
certain members of the
caucasian race.)

The second is to run rapidly
in another direction.
Polite poets do not run,
throw up, or strike
the other person in a conversation.
What we do is let our minds ramble.

So nodding in the appropriate places
I left the bar
traveled
first to the sixties
back to the cramped living rooms
activist dykes
consciousness-raising sessions
I polled the women there
one by one
Is this what it was all about?
Did we brave the wrath of threatened bar owners.
so women could wear handkerchiefs in their pockets?
one by one I asked.
Their faces faded
furrows of frowns on their brows
I went to the halls
where we sat hours upon hours
arguing with Gay men
trying to build a united movement
I polled the people there
one by one

Is this why we did it?
Did we grapple with our own who hated us

so women could use whips and chains?
The faces faded
puzzled faces drift out of vision.
I returned to the jails
where women sat bruised and beaten
singing songs of liberation
through puffed lips
I polled the women there
one by one
Is this why we did it?
Did we take to the streets
so women can carve swastikas on their bodies?

Hundreds and hundreds of women
pass by
no, march by
chant, sing, cry
I return to the voice
the young voice in the bar
and I am angry
the vision of women playing
as Nazis, policeman, rapists
taunts me
mocks me
words drift through

it's always by consent
we are oppressed by other dykes
who don't understand
and I am back in the bar
furious

the poll is complete
no, no no no
this is not why we did it
this is not why we continue to do.

We need not play at being victim
we need not practice pain
we need not encourage helplessness
they lurk outside of doors
follow us through the streets
and claim our lives daily.
We must not offer haven
for fascists and pigs
be it real or fantasy
the line is too unclear.

GEORGIA, GEORGIA GEORGIA ON MY MIND

I

It came at first
like a rumor
traveling through
Black pages
of *Jet* and *Ebony*
children are missing
children are dead
in a southern metropolis
the common denominator
Black and young.

It comes again
now a nasty gnawing truth
Black bodies float up
from rivers and ditches
each week
more missing
more dead.

II

Now let the circus begin.
Proper politicians
come to town
reporters run from

family to family
look and see
the crying mother
at her child's funeral
look and see
the scared commissioners
'We're doing all we can.'

III

Fear raises its head
the unspoken belief
the killers
white,
the Klan, the Nazis
maniacs, crazies
genocide
eliminate the young
stop the breeding
Black friends angry
bitter scream
'those lousy bastards'
'those racist fiends'
white friends afraid
better to be quiet
and hope it's one insane fool.

IV

The lessons are
slowly slipped out

it's a shame *but*
if the kids were
not in the streets
Mother
why weren't you home
with your child?
the President says
he'll send more money for
investigation
two weeks after he
announced his budget cuts
the police psychologist
swears the killers
are Black
'the kids wouldn't trust
a white'
and half the nation prays
he's right.

My anger rises
I know who the killers are
and how the killer will go untried
see no court or judges
no jury or peers
the killers wear the suits of
businessmen
buy ghetto apartments
and overcharge the rent
the killers lock Black men
in prison or drive
them from their homes

the killers give the Black woman
a job
and pay her one-half of what she
needs to live
the killers scream about
juvenile crime
and refuse to build child-care centers.
it won't matter what
demented fool is caught
for society has provided
the lure.

A rich kid is not tempted
by candy
a rich kid is not tempted
by movies
a rich kid is not tempted
by attention.
Long after the murders of
Atlanta are solved
the killer will remain free.

ONE THANKSGIVING DAY

One Thanksgiving Day
Priscilla Ford
got into her
Lincoln Continental
drove to Virginia Street
in downtown Reno
and ran over thirty people.
Six of them died.

One Thanksgiving Day
Priscilla Ford
got into her
Lincoln Continental
drove to Virginia Street
in downtown Reno
and ran over thirty people.
Six of them died.

Priscilla, Priscilla
who did you see?
what face from your past?
Was it the waitress
who waited to wait
on you?
Was it the clerk
who tried to sell you
only the
brightest colored clothes?

Was it your child's
teacher who tried to
teach her that she was
slow?
Was it the security guard
at the bank who guarded
you from the bank's money
with his eyes?
One Thanksgiving Day
Priscilla Ford
got into her
Lincoln Continental
drove to Virginia Street
in downtown Reno
and ran over thirty people.
Six of them died.

Screams filled the street
Panic ran through the crowd
like a losing streak
at the blackjack tables
and the state of Nevada
was stunned
A tired middle-aged Black woman
was not thankful that day
not thankful for her job
wrapping gifts at Macy's
not thankful for the state
taking custody of her child
she was not thankful
for her Lincoln Continental.

Priscilla Ford
got into her Lincoln Continental
and hurled through the streets of Reno
the killer made in Motown factories
swept down on tourists
looking to make a big hit
hit by a navy blue
steel bludgeon
screams dying beneath its wheels
and the state of Nevada
was angry.

She went to trial.
Insanity
her lawyers pled
she was crazy with anger
she was crazy with fear
she was crazy with defeat
she was crazy with isolation
no sane person kills
strangers with their cars
Priscilla Ford said yes
I drove my car
into the whiteness
of Nevada streets
she would say nothing more
and the state of Nevada
was frightened.
If Priscilla Ford could do it
who else?

How many Black faces
that emptied garbage
waited tables
bagged groceries
wrapped presents
were capable?

Reaction was swift.
One entrepreneur
printed a card
it said *Happy Thanksgiving*
with a picture of Priscilla
on its front
inside it said
Sorry I Missed YOU.

Priscilla Ford
got into her
Lincoln Continental
drove down Virginia Street
in downtown Reno
and ran over thirty people.
Six of them died
and the state of Nevada
was vindictive.
You cannot be insane
to be enraged is not insane
to be filled with hatred is not insane
to lash out at whiteness is not insane
it is being a nigger
it is your place in life.

Priscilla Ford
got into her
Lincoln Continental
drove to Virginia Street
in downtown Reno
and ran over thirty people.
Six of them died
and now Priscilla Ford
will die.
The state of Nevada
has judged

that it is
not crazy
for Black folks
to kill white folks
with their cars.

Priscilla Ford
will be
the second woman
executed in Nevada's history.
it's her highest
finish in life.

JONESTOWN

As a child in Texas
race education
was simple
was subtle
was sharp

The great lone star
state sharply
placed me
in colored schools
with colored teachers
and colored books
and colored knowledge

I shopped in white stores
and bought colored clothes
'Keep the colors loud and bright
so they dazzle in the night
No matter where a nigger's bred
they love yellow, orange and red'

I used colored toilets
and rode colored buses home
I went to colored churches
with colored preachers
and prayed to a white God
begged forgiveness for Cain
and his sins
and his descendants

us lowly colored sinners
and the message
was simple
was sharp
there is a place for niggers
but not among good white folk

At home
race education
was simple
was subtle
fact gleaned
by differences

The white man
who jumped
free-fall
in the sky
was quietly dismissed
'white folks are crazy'
the white man
who turned
somersaults
on Sports Spectacular skis
was quietly dismissed
'white folks will do anything
for money'
the white man who
shot and killed his wife
and children
and then himself

received a headshake
and a sigh
and the simple statement
'white folks are crazy'

And the messages
fell into place
white folks went crazy
and went to nut houses
Black folks got mad
and went to jail
white folks owned America
Black folks built it

As I grew into adulthood
many messages were discarded
many were forgotten
but one returns to haunt me

Black folks do not commit suicide
Black folks do not
Black folks do not
Black folks do not commit suicide

November 18, 1978
more than 900 people
most of them Black
died in a man-made town
called Jonestown

Newscaster's words
slap me in my face

peoples' tears and grief
emanate from my set
and I remember the lessons
rehear a childhood message

Black folks do not commit suicide

I thought of my uncle Dave
he died in prison
suicide
the authorities said
'Boy just up and hung hisself'
and I remember my mother
her disbelief, her grief
'Them white folks kilt my brother
Dave didn't commit no suicide'
and the funeral
a bitter quiet funeral
his coffin sealed from sighters
and we all knew
Dave died not by his hands
some guard decided
that nigger should die

And I stare at the newscaster
he struggles to contain himself
it's a BIG BIG story
and he must not
seem too excited

'American troops made a
grizzly discovery today

in Jonestown, Guyana'
my innards scream as
the facts unfold
'a communist preacher'
and I see old Black women
my grandmothers
communist NO
little old Black ladies
do not believe in communists
they believe in God
and Jesus yet,
the newscasters' words
a *commune*
a media storm of
words and pictures
interviews with ex-members
survivors, city officials

the *San Francisco Chronicle*
had a problem with its presses
erratic delivery
of the morning paper
and in two days the *Chronicle*
publishes a book
Eyewitness Account
by a staff reporter
who survived
the airport attack
and the story grows
STEP RIGHT UP
STEP RIGHT UP

Ladies and Gentlemen
have I got a tale
for you
we got these men
two men
a congressman & a preacher
& a supporting cast of hundreds
the congressman went
to investigate the preacher
and wound up dead
the preacher wound up dead
the supporting cast
wound up dead
and all the dead
are singing to me

Black folks do not
Black folks do not
Black folks do not commit suicide
My phone rings
newscaster mistakenly says
Patricia *Parker*
not *Parks*
died on the airstrip
a friend
wants to know
are you alive?

Yes
I am here
not there festering

in a jungle
with bloated belly
not a victim
in a dream deferred
not a piece
in a media puzzle
not a member
in the supporting cast.

Yet
I am there
walking with the souls
of Black folks
crying
screaming
WHYWHY
Black folks
why are you here
and dead?
tell me how you
willingly died
did the minister
sing to you
'Kool-aid Kool-aid
taste great
I like Kool-aid
can't wait'

I see Black people
beautiful Black people
in lines in front of a tub

of twentieth-century hemlock
I see guards with guns
guns   guns
why guns?
and the pictures
continue to flow
images of a man
a church man
he cures disease
NO
he's a fake
hired people
treated liver
he loves God
NO
he's a communist
he talks many messages
revolution to the young
God to the old
he believes in the family
NO
he destroys the family
fucks the women
fucks the men
and the media continues
to tell the tale

An interview with a live one.
'You were a member of the People's Temple?'
'Yes, I was.'
'Why did you join?'

'Well, I went there a few times
and then I stopped going, but
Rev. Jones came by my house
and asked me why I quit coming.
I was really surprised.
No one had ever cared
that much about me before.'

No one had ever cared
that much about me before
and it came home
the messages of my youth
came clear
the Black people
in Jonestown
did not commit suicide
they were murdered
they were murderedin
small southern towns
they were murdered in
big northern cities

they were murdered
as school children
by teachers
who didn't care
there were murdered
by policemen
who didn't care
they were murdered
by welfare workers

who didn't care
by shopkeepers
who didn't care
they were murdered
by church people
who didn't care
they were murdered
by politicians
who didn't care
they didn't die at Jonestown
they went to Jonestown dead
convinced that America
and Americans
didn't care

they died
in the schoolrooms
they died
in the streets
they died
in the bars
they died
in the jails
they died
in the churches they died
in the welfare lines

Jim Jones was not the cause
he was the result
of 400 years
of not caring

Black folks do not
Black folks do not
Black do not commit suicide

LEGACY

for Anastasia Jean

'Anything handed down from,
or as from an ancestor to a descendant.'

Prologue

There are those who think
or perhaps don't think
that children and lesbians
together can't make a family
that we create an extension
of perversion.

They think
or perhaps don't think
that we have different relationships
with our children
that instead of getting up
in the middle of the night
for a 2 AM and 6 AM feeding
we rise up and chant
'you're gonna be a dyke
you're gonna be a dyke.'

That we feed our children
lavender Similac
and by breathing our air

the children's genitals distort
and they become hermaphrodites.

They ask
'What will you say to them
what will you teach them?'

Child
that would be mine
I bring you my world and
bid it be yours.'

I
Addie and George

He was a small man
son of an African slave
his father came chained
in a boat
long after the boats
had 'stopped' coming
his skin was ebony
shone like new piano keys.

He was a carpenter
worked long in the trade
of the christ he chose
six days a week
his hands plied the wood
gave birth to houses
and cabinets and tables
on the seventh day

he lay down his hammer
and picked up his bible
and preached the gospel
to his brethren
led his flock in prayer

when he was seventy-nine years old
he lay down
in the presence of his wife
and children
and died.

Her father too was a slave
common law wed to an indian squaw
Addie came colored caramel
long black hair
high cheek bones.

She was a christian woman
her religion a daily occurrence
her allegiance was to God,
her husband, her children
in that order
together she and George
had twenty-two children
many never survived
the first year of life
a fact not unusual
for the time.

When she was seventy-six
George died

she began to travel
to the homes of her children
to make sure they led
a christian life
the children hid
their beer and bourbon
the grandchildren hid
she would come for two months
then move on
leave the words of Jehovah
sweating from the walls
when she was ninety-four years old
she lay down
and died.

II
Ernest and Marie

He came from the earth, they say,
an expression meaning *orphan*
parents in the hands of poverty
best give the boy away
and so he came to live
in a good christian home
with a good christian minister
and his wife
he was a man of many trades
roofer in the summer
tire retreader in the winter
earned far beyond
his four years of education

he wanted to see
all of his children
get educated
he lived long enough to see
his children gone and grown
and then
he lay low
and died.

She was the youngest of the twenty-two
quiet woman
tall for her time
she bore eight children
five survived the early years
she raised them in a christian way
by day she cleaned houses
by night she cleaned her own
she was sixty-two when her husband died
took her first plane trip that same year
when her third daughter was killed
she cremated her child and went home
willed herself sick and weary
she took three years to complete the task
then she lay down
and died.

III

It is from this past that I come
surrounded by sisters in blood
and spirit

it is this past
that I bequeath
a history of work and struggle.

Each generation improves the world
for the next.
My grandparents willed me strength.
My parents willed me pride.
I will to you rage.
I give you a world incomplete
a world where
women still
are property and chattel
where
color still
shuts doors
where
sexual choice still
threatens
but I give you
a legacy
of doers
of people who take risks
to chisel the crack wider.

Take the strength that you may
wage a long battle.
Take the pride that you can
never stand small.
Take the rage that you can
never settle for less.

These be the things I pass
to you my daughter

if this is the result of perversion
let the world stand screaming.
You will mute their voices
with your life.

MY BROTHER

for Blackberri

I

It is a simple ritual.
Phone rings
Berri's voice
low, husky
'What's you're doing?'
'Not a thing,
you coming over?'
'Well, I thought I'd
come by."
A simple ritual.
He comes
we eat
watch television
play cards
play video games
some nights
he sleeps over
others
he goes home
sometimes
he brings a friend
more often
he doesn't.
A simple ritual.

II

It's a pause that alerts me
tells me this time
is hard time
the pain has risen
to the water line
we rarely verbalize
there is no need.

Within this lifestyle
there is much to undo you.

Hey look at the faggot!
When I was a child
our paper boy was Claude
every day
seven days a week
he bared the Texas weather
the rain that never stopped
walked through the Black section
where sidewalks had not
yet been invented
and ditches filled with water.
Walk careful Claude
across the plank
that serves as sidewalk
sometime tips into the murky water
or heat
wet heat
that covers your pores

cascades rivulets of
stinging sweat down your body.
Our paper boy Claude
bared the weather well
each day he came
and each Saturday at dusk
he would come to collect.

My parents liked Claude.
Each Saturday Claude polite
would come
always said thank you
whether we had the money
or not.
Each Saturday
my father would say
Claude is a nice boy
works hard
goes to church
gives money to his mother
and each Sunday
we would go to Church
and there would be Claude
in his choir robes
til the Sunday
when he didn't come.

Hey look at the faggot!

Some young men howled at him
ran in a pack

reverted to some ancient form
they took Claude
took his money
yelled faggot
as they cast his body
in front of a car.

III

How many cars have you dodged Berri?
How many ancient young men have you met?
Perhaps your size saved you
but then you were not always this size
perhaps your fleetness
perhaps
there are no more ancient young men.

Ah!   Within this lifestyle
we have chosen.
Sing?
What do you mean
you wanna be a singer?
Best get a good government job
maybe sing on the side.
You heard the words:
Be responsible
Be respectable
Be stable
Be secure
Be normal, boy.

How many quarter-filled rooms
have you sang your soul to
then washed away with
blended whiskey?

I told my booking agent one year
book me a tour
Blackberri and I
will travel this land
together
take our Black Queerness
into the face
of this place and say

Hey, here we are
a faggot & a dyke, Black
we make good music
& write good poems
We Be—Something Else.

My agent couldn't book us.
It seemed my lesbian audiences
were not ready for my faggot
brother
and I remembered
a law conference
in San Francisco
where women
women who loved women
threw boos and tomatoes

at a women who dared
to have a man in her band.

What is this world we have?
is my house the only safe place
for us?
And I am rage
all the low-paying gigs
all the uncut records
all the dodged cars
all the fear escaping
all the unclaimed love
so I could offer my bosom
and food
and shudder
fearful of the time
when it will not be
enough
fearful of the time
when the ritual
ends.

from
Uncollected Poems

TRYING TO DO HOW MAMA DID CAN UN DO YOU

Prologue

I don't know about you,
I know about me—
I remember— as a child
watching my mama—
and I came to certain
Conclusions.
Her life was not going
to be mine—
Call it childish clarity
or aimful ambition
one thing for certain
I wasn't going to be like my mama,
What I didn't know
couldn't seem to see—there was
no way that could ever be
Now I have to admit
with a lot more respect
Trying to do how mama did it
can undo you.

I.

Trying to do
How mama did
Can undo you

Remember when she said
some day you'll
mark my words

I remember
Mama used to
work washing floors
Then she came home
and cooked dinner
and cleaned house
and was mama

That's simple stuff
until you do it

I, first realized
Mama's power
I tried
to cook a
pot of gumbo

Gumbo—
a southern
dish consisting
of seafood,
sausage, okra, and
chicken, served
over rice—
a working class
bouillabaise

Mama's gumbo
drove me nuts
I couldn't get
it dirty—
Could NOT find
that dishwater look

Mama didn't believe
in writing recipes
called her up once
and asked—
how do I cook this?
Well daughter,
you take a
pinch of this
and a little
less than a
handful of that
and a smidgen
of . . .
I tried though
Got 2nd degree burns
from hot water cornbread –
ruined a whole sack of
potatoes trying to get
sweet potato salad –
and biscuits and gravy . . .
Trying to do
how mama
did can
un Do
you

II.

Mama used
to be off on Tuesday
I'd come from

school and the
house would be
gleaming—
Food on the stove— And
all the drawers
filled with
fresh washed,
clothes—
Closets filled
with ironed
and starched
blouses and
dresses,
immaculate—

At first she washed
by hand — a
scrub board and
a tin tub
later — She got
a washer—
finger type—
never did use
a dryer
except the sun.

I tried, mama
I got up early on my
day off— Gathered
the clothes—
Loaded the washer
Then swept all
the floors — broke

out the mop & 409 —
the oven cleaner —
the sponges —
Mama used
to make her
own soap
Put the second
load in the washer
Folded the first
Started scrubbing
the kitchen cabinets —
Mama used to
scrub all the
walls— wash
the venetian blinds
and can fruits &
vegetables on
her day off
I got the kitchen cleaned—
smiled at me like
Sun on a waxed fender
but it was 1 o'clock
and I was exhausted—
Trying to do
like mama did
can undo you

III.

After work,
She'd come home

cook dinner and
wait on Daddy
hand and foot

A man's home
is his castle, child
keep it well and
he won't stray

When I first got married
I'd run home from work
Cook dinner —
but after a while
that got too tacky

He wanted ironed
shirts, starched.
Dinner ready at
7. And wanted
me to go to bed
with him too.

Mama used
to iron the sheets
and Daddy's shorts
too.

I finally decided
that either mama
was an amazon
or nuts or
Daddy was crazy
but my old man had to go.

Trying to do
like mama did
can undo you

IV.

I like kids,
I love my daughter
but sometimes —
She drives me nuts

Mama had 8
kids — 3
died in childhood

At least once,
every other week
the kid runs out
of socks or panties—
or they get lost—
I don't know how
but she loses them

Every Tuesday
all our clothes
were put in
our drawers
for the week
socks matched –
on the right
underwear
on the left.
ironed blouses
folded in
the middle.

I try to cook
balanced meals
but sometimes

I have to break
out the hot dogs
and chili – or
get pizza or
Kentucky fried –
I'm just too
whipped to cook.

Mama raised
five – I had
my first take out
food when I was 17
on a trip to California

V.

"It's nice to be
nice"

I hated that expression
when my sisters took my things
and I took revenge

"It's nice to be
nice"

When my friends broke my toys
and I tried to break their faces

"It's nice to be
nice"

When my father punished
me for nothing–and I
sulked for 3 days.

“It’s nice to be
nice”

I decided one week
to do like mama
did—
no matter what was said,
no matter what deed done,
I would respond with kindness

I got a parking ticket—
The bank lost my paycheck—
My fender got crushed
in the parking lot,
when I started parking
to avoid getting any more
parking tickets.
I got cut in front of,
in the supermarket line.
I started getting an
ulcer—
Decided to respond
in kind—

Trying to do
like mama did—
can un do you

What’s certain for sure
is I am not my mama—
Things she did—
I cannot do—

but I do a few things
Mama couldn't do
She never saw a subway
or knew how to fend off a pass
or balance a check book
or tell a racist to
kiss her ass

Yeah—mama and I
are different folk
move through life
in stranger ways
but I've always
loved her
and now I
know—respect
is due her
for the way she did—
I'm a witness
these facts are true
Trying to do—
like mama did
can undo you.

BRICK HUT

Pat Parker wrote the lyrics to this song recorded by Mary Watkins

What do you do when your love is gone?
Left you and the kittens sittin' all alone
Grab your hiking boots and your coverall
Your fashion best from St Vincent de Paul
Comb your hair, get out your ride
Go get a sammich, it's the place –
Brick Hut
Shake your gloom, get out your room
At the Brick Hut
Brick Hut
Yeah
At the Brick Hut

It's always crowded, got to wait for a seat
But watching the people is some kind of treat
They got hippies, hobos, kids and babes
Everything from drinks to scrambled eggs
Just a place to shake your gloom
Like being in a shrink's waiting room
Shake your gloom, get out your room
At the Brick Hut
Brick Hut
At the Brick Hut

Get rid of sadness, break out of your shell
Go to the hut, check out the person there

If you're bored and need a change of pace
Stop by the Hut and meet a new face
Shake it, shake it, shake it
Shake it, shake it, shake it
Shake it, shake it, shake it
Get rid of sadness, break out of your shell
Go to the Hut, check out the person there
If you're bored and need a change of pace
Stop by the Hut and meet a new face
Shake it, shake it
Shake it, shake it
Shake it, shake it
At the Brick Hut, yeah
Shake it, shake it Shake it, shake it Shake it, shake it At the Brick Hut, yeah
Shake it, shake it Shake it, shake it Shake it, shake it At the Brick Hut, yeah
Shake it, shake it Shake it, shake it Shake it, shake it

"Brick Hut" is the third track on Mary Watkins's album *Something Moving* (Olivia Records, 1978). Thanks to J.D. Doyle for highlighting that Pat Parker wrote the lyrics. For more information: https://www.queermusicheritage.com/olivia-mw.html.

Speech

REVOLUTION: IT'S NOT NEAT OR PRETTY OR QUICK

The following speech was given at the BASTA conference in Oakland, California, in August 1980. It represented three organizations: The Black Women's Revolutionary Council, the Eleventh Hour Battalion, and The Feminist Women's Health Center in Oakland.

I have been to many conferences: People's Constitutional Convention in Washington, DC, Women's Conference on Violence in San Francisco, Lesbian Conference in Los Angeles, International Tribunal on Crimes Against Women in Belgium. I've been to more conferences than I can name and to many I would like to forget, but I have never come to a conference with as much anticipation and feeling of urgency.

We are in a critical time. Imperialist forces in the world are finding themselves backed against the wall; no longer able to control the world with the threat of force. And they are getting desperate. And they should be desperate. What we do here this weekend and what we take from this conference can be the difference, the deciding factor as to whether a group of women will ever again be able to meet not only in this country, but the entire world. We are facing the most critical time in the history of the world. The super- powers cannot afford for us to join forces and work to rid this earth of them, and we cannot afford not to.

In order to leave here prepared to be a strong force in the fight against imperialism we must have a clear understanding of what imperialism is and how it manifests itself in our lives. It is perhaps easier for us to understand the nature of imperialism when we look at how this country deals with other countries. It doesn't take a great amount of political sophistication to see how the interest of oil companies played a role in our relationship with the Shah's Iran. The people of Iran were exploited in order for Americans to drive gas-guzzling monsters. And that is perhaps the difficult part of imperialism for us to understand.

The rest of the world is being exploited in order to maintain our standard of living. We who are five percent of the world's population use forty percent of the world's oil.

As anti-imperialists we must be prepared to destroy all imperialist governments, and we must realize that by doing this we will drastically alter the standard of living that we now enjoy. We cannot talk on one hand about making revolution in this country, yet be unwilling to give up our videotape records and recreational vehicles. An anti-imperialist understands the exploitation of the working class, understands that in order for capitalism to function, there must be a certain percentage that is unemployed. We must also define our friends and enemies based on their stand on imperialism.

At this time, the super powers are in a state of decline. The Iranians rose up and said no to U. S. imperialism; the Afghanis and Eritreans are saying no to Soviet-social imperialism. The situation has become critical and the only resource left is world war between the U.S. and the Soviet Union. We are daily being given warning that war is imminent. To some people, this is no significant change, just escalation. The Blacks, poor whites, Chicanos, and other oppressed people of this country already know we're at war.

And the rest of the country's people are being prepared. The media is bombarding us with patriotic declarations about "our" hostages and "our" embassy in Iran. This government is constantly reminding us of our commitment to our allies in Israel. Ads inviting us to become the few, the chosen, the marine or fly with the air force, etc. are filling our television screens.

And it doesn't stop there. This system is insidious in its machinations. It's no coincidence that the "right wing" of this country is being mobilized. Media sources are bombarding us with the news of KKK and Nazi party activity. But we who were involved in the civil rights movement are very familiar with these tactics. We remember the revelations of FBI agents, not only infiltrating the Klan but participating in and leading their activities. And we are not for one moment fooled by these manipulations.

The Klan and the Nazis are our enemies and must be stopped, but to simply mobilize around stopping them is not enough. They are functionaries, tools of this governmental system. They serve in the same ways as our armed forces and police. To end Klan or Nazi activity doesn't end imperialism. It doesn't end institutional racism; it doesn't end sexism; it does not bring this monster down, and we must not forget what our goals are and who our enemies are. To simply label these people as lunatic fringes and not accurately assess their roles as a part of this system is a dangerous error. These people do the dirty work. They are the arms and legs of the congressmen, the businessmen, the Tri-lateral Commission.

And the message they bring is coming clear. Be a good American—support registration for the draft. The equation is being laid out in front of us. Good American = support imperialism and war.

To this, I must declare—I am not a good American. I do not wish to have the world colonized, bombarded and plundered in order to eat steak.

Each time a national liberation victory is won I applaud and support it. It means we are one step closer to ending the madness that we live under. It means we weaken the chains that are binding the world.

Yet to support national liberation struggles alone is not enough. We must actively fight within the confines of this country to bring it down. I am not prepared to let other nationalities do my dirty work for me. I want the people of Iran to be free. I want the people of Puerto Rico to be free, but I am a revolutionary feminist because I want me to be free. And it is critically important to me that you who are here, that your commitment to revolution is based on the fact that you want revolution for yourself.

In order for revolution to be possible, and revolution is possible, it must be led by the poor and working class people of this country. Our interest does not lie with being a part of this system, and our tendencies to be coopted and diverted are lessened by the realization of our oppression. We know and understand that our oppression is not simply a question of nationality but that poor and working class people are oppressed throughout the world by the imperialist powers.

The issues of women are the issues of the working class as well. By not having this understanding, the women's movement has allowed itself to be co-opted and misdirected.

It is unthinkable to me as a revolutionary feminist that some women's liberationist would entertain the notion that women should be drafted in exchange for passage of the ERA. This is a clear example of not understanding imperialism and not basing one's political line on its destruction. If the passage of the ERA means that I am going to become an equal participant in the exploitation of the world; that I am going to bear arms against other Third World people who are fighting to reclaim what is rightfully theirs—then I say Fuck the ERA.

One of the difficult questions for us to understand is just "what is revolution?" Perhaps we have had too many years of media madness with "revolutionary eye make-up and revolutionary tampons." Perhaps we have had too many years of Hollywood fantasy where the revolutionary man kills his enemies and walks off into the sunset with his revolutionary woman who has been waiting for his return. And that's the end of the tale.

The reality is that revolution is not a one-step process: you fight—you win—it's over. It takes years. Long after the smoke of the last gun has faded away the struggle to build a society that is classless, that has no traces of sexism and racism in it, will still be going on. We have many examples of societies in our lifetime that have had successful armed revolution. And we have no examples of any country that has completed the revolutionary process. Is Russia now the society that Marx and Lenin dreamed? Is China the society that Mao dreamed? Before and after armed revolution there must be education, and analysis, and struggle. If not, and even if so, one will be faced with coups, counter-revolution and revision.

The other illusion is that revolution is neat. It's not neat or pretty or quick. It is a long dirty process. We will be faced with decisions that are not easy. We will have to consider the deaths of friends and family. We will be faced with the decisions of killing members of our own race.

Another illusion that we suffer under in this country is that a single facet of the population can make revolution. Black people alone cannot make a revolution in this country. Native American people alone cannot make revolution in this country. Chicanos alone cannot make revolution in this country. White people alone cannot make revolution in this country. Women alone cannot make revolution in this country. Gay people alone cannot make revolution in this country. And anyone who tries it will not be successful.

Yet it is critically important for women to take a leadership role in this struggle. And I do not mean leading the way to the coffee machine.

A part of the task charged to us this weekend is deciding the direction we must take. First I say let us reclaim our movement. For too long I have watched the white middle class be represented as my leaders in the women's movement. I have often heard that the women's movement is a white middle class movement.

I am a feminist. I am neither white nor middle class. And the women that I've worked with were like me. Yet I am told that we don't exist, and that we didn't exist. Now I understand that the racism and classism of some women in the movement prevented them from seeing me and people like me. But I also understand that with the aid of the media many middle class women were made more visible. And this gave them an opportunity to use their skills gained through their privilege to lead the movement into at first reformist and now counter-revolutionary bullshit.

These women allowed themselves to be red-baited and dyke-baited into isolating and ignoring the progressive elements of the women's movement. And I, for one, am no longer willing to watch a group of self-serving reformist idiots continue to abort the demands of revolutionary thinking women. You and I are the women's movement. It's leadership and direction should come from us.

We are charged with the task of rebuilding and revitalizing the dreams of the 60s and turning it into the reality of the 80s. And it will not be easy. At the same time that we must weed reformist elements out of our movement we will have to fight tooth and nail with our brothers and sisters of the left. For in reality, we are "all products of a decadent capitalist society."

At the same time that we must understand and support the men and women of national liberation struggles—the left must give up its undying loyalty to the nuclear family. In the same way it is difficult for upper and middle class women to give up their commitment to the nuclear family, but the nuclear family is the basic unit of capitalism and in order for us to move to revolution it has to be destroyed. And I mean destroyed. The male left has duped too many women with cries of genocide into believing it is revolutionary to be bound to babies. As to the question of abortion, I am appalled at the presumptions of men. The question is whether or not we have control of our bodies which in turn means control of our community and its growth. I believe that Black women are as intelligent as white women and we know when to have babies or not. And I want no man regardless of color to tell me when and where to bear children. As long as women are bound by the nuclear family structure we cannot effectively move toward revolution. And if women don't move, it will not happen.

We do not have an easy task before us. At this conference we will disagree; we will get angry; we will fight. This is good and should be welcomed. Here is where we should air our differences but here is also where we should build. In order to survive in this world we must make a commitment to change it; not reform it—revolutionize it. Here is where we begin to build a new women's movement, not one easily co-opted and misdirected by media pigs and agents of this insidious imperialist system. Here is where we begin to build a revolutionary force of women. Judy Grahn in the "She Who" poems says, "When she who moves, the earth will turn over." You and I are the she who and if we dare to struggle, dare to win, this earth will turn over.

"Revolution: It's Not Neat or Pretty or Quick," was first delivered as a speech as indicated in the head note; this transcription first appeared in *This Bridge Called My Back: Writings by Radical Women of Color*, in 1983.

You might also enjoy…

Pat Parker was born in Houston, TX, in 1944 and moved to Los Angeles, CA after she graduated high school. She lived in the San Francisco bay area from 1965 until her death. Parker died in 1989 from complications of cancer. Her partner of nine years, Martha Dunham, and their daughter, Anastasia Dunham-Parker-Brady, survived her as well as Cassidy Brown who she co-parented.

SaraEllen Strongman is an interdisciplinary scholar and assistant professor of Afroamerican and African Studies at the University of Michigan.

Sapphic Classics from *Sinister Wisdom*

Alexis De Veaux *Blue Heat*
Anita Cornwell *Black Lesbian in White America*
Chocolate Waters *Melting in Your Mouth*

Order online at
www.sinisterwisdom.org
Or mail check or money order to:
Sinister Wisdom - 2333 McIntosh Road
Dover, FL 33527-5980

Order Sapphic Classics from your local bookseller through IPG book distribution or directly from *Sinister Wisdom* at www.sinisterwisdom.org/SapphicClassics